C000280208

Dunmow

in old picture postcards

by
Stan Jarvis

European Library – Zaltbommel/Netherlands

Third edition: 1994

GB   ISBN 90 288 3417 6 / CIP

© 1986 European Library – Zaltbommel/Netherlands

No part of this book may be reproduced in any form, by print, photoprint, microfilm or any other means, without written permission from the publisher.

INTRODUCTION

The word Dunmow has been used in this book to embrace the two parishes of Great and Little Dunmow, but the postcards shown cannot be said to have been provided in any proportion to the relative size of the places. It is quite understandable that by far the most postcards have been produced of Great Dunmow because it has always been the 'big brother' of the two, with the shops and services, and the main roads which bring the travellers and the tourists. A guide book in circulation at the beginning of the century, when many of the photographs were taken, speaks of Great Dunmow as: 'A considerable market town (Tuesday) situated on the Chelmer... It consists of two main streets.' Little Dunmow, says the same guide, is noted largely for the custom of '...presenting a Flitch of Bacon to any couple who, sleeping or waking, had not repented of their marriage for a year and a day. The applicants were required to swear a poetical oath, kneeling on some sharp stones at the church door, which stones are now preserved in the vestry...'

As to the origin of the postcards, Great Dunmow tradesmen were as enterprising as their big-town brethren; they saw the cyclists and the trippers come pouring out from London on their fresh air forays, looking for rural peace and verdant views and they were ready for them with their souvenir postcards. Newsagents, tobacconists and stationers like Willett's, Stacey's, and Dowsett's offered a surprising variety. And very often those postcards were not posted, but kept as reminders of happy days in the Dunmow district, so they carry no postmark which would have helped to attribute a date.

Problems of identification of places, people and period have been overcome through the kind and generous help I have received from so many people in Dunmow. Chief among the contributors of cards to my collection is the Essex Record Office. Mr. and Mrs. Mackenzie lent me many cards from their precious family archives and supported them with much useful information. Mr. and Mrs. Byford together were a mine of information. They not only lent me their precious and frighteningly fragile glass negatives and gave me a full description of the views represented but also put me in touch with other helpful old inhabitants of Dunmow.

Naturally the author of a prospective book of photographs would turn to the local photographer for help. Dunmow's present-day and very professional photographer David Lipson's interest, advice and generous help in the long term loan of many photographs he has produced from old postcards through years of service to the town is very much appreciated. Mr. Beard and Mrs. Barham were kind enough to get in touch with me and offer the one or two postcards and commentary which were as important as the last pieces in a jigsaw puzzle. Last but not least, the ladies of Dunmow's Inner Wheel showed such a warm and friendly interest in this project. I thank all these kind people, from the heart. My old friend Geoff Baker knows how very much his help is appreciated.

Great Dunmow is that delightful paradox – a town in the country. Its inhabitants are envied by those Essex people who have to live in vast conurbations or on dreary dormitory estates. In Dunmow any able-bodied person can walk from the countryside through the town into open countryside again, in any direction. Modern building in the town has been sympathetic with the existing townscape which is so attractive through the preservation of its old shop fronts. The capacious car park and the supermarket have been concealed cunningly from the view of the main street. It is small wonder that many families can boast of a long association with the area. Little Dunmow's main street has not altered a jot over sixty years, though there has been building and rebuilding around the village to provide more homes.

No doubt it was a wrench for the Romans when they were recalled to their homeland, but some of them had already lived their lives in Dunmow and their cremated burial remains have been found at Merks Hill, High Style and Springfields. The Saxons liked the look of the place, 'the meadow on the hill' as they called it in their language, and the name stuck, as Dunmow, down to this day.

At Domesday the place was comprised of the seven manors formerly belonging to the Saxon lords. From the Norman takeover Dunmow quietly progressed through to the thirteenth century when it was granted a weekly market and an annual fair by Henry III. The important charter of 1555 afforded the busy little town borough status. It had to yield up that reputation in Victorian times because it was not big enough to be classed as one of the new boroughs, but Dunmow was not greatly disturbed; it simply carried on its age-old activities as market place, shopping and administrative centre for a wide area of farmland interspersed with villages and hamlets.

In this way the Dunmows continue to this day – a refreshingly unspoilt town and a village in the heart of pleasant Essex countryside. I dedicate this book to the people of Dunmow – who are well aware of their good fortune, and to my wife Hazel, a truly constant companion.

DUNMOW. 764.

1. The problem of looking after sick and poor people was, by the end of the eighteenth century, beyond the resources of individual parishes, so twenty-five of them, centred on Dunmow, joined together to build and run the 'Union Workhouse' as a home and a hospital for less fortunate inhabitants. It was put up in 1840 in red brick with white brick window openings and black diaper patterns borrowed from the Tudor period. This postcard was produced by Fred Spalding of Chelmsford about 1910 when Master and Matron of the Workhouse were William Errington and his wife. Even by the advent of the Great War it was obsolescent and was used to house German prisoners of war. Before the last war it was sold to a private developer and has been transformed into a number of prestigious flats.

2. On the right as the visitor went townwards was the railway station seen here. There is now no trace of it at all; new industrial units cover the site. In 1910 it was '… a station on the Bishops Stortford, Dunmow and Braintree line of the Great Eastern Railway'. In 1864 some six thousand people flocked to see Lady Henniker of Newton Hall cut the first sod with a silver spade from a spot below New Street. 'An omnibus meets every train,' says the Directory of the day; there was a day, however, when it did not – 'A singular accident to a 'bus occurred at Dunmow Station on Tuesday. The vehicle was standing outside the station when the horse, becoming frightened at some pigs, bolted into the cattle yard. In the 'bus were Mrs. Priestman and her child. Seeing the danger of the horse plunging down on the dock metals, Porter Reeve jumped into the vehicle and pulled the lady out… Mr. Priestman had just time to sieze the little one as the horse plunged over the precipitous dock wall and the 'bus crashed on its side to the metals…' (Essex Weekly News, 11th September, 1908.)

3. The road continued up the hill to the junction with the Braintree road. On the left the fields were developed to house the Dunmow Flitch Bacon Company, not even proposed until 1908 and now demolished. The railway sidings which served the factory have been replaced by the Dunmow bypass which takes so much of the modern motor traffic clear of the town. On the right at the junction is Park Corner, reminder that the parkland of Dunmow Park estate, seen at the extreme right of the postcard, came up this far. The Braintree road, running into the background, is still called Stane Street on maps today, showing that it began as one of the Romans' paved highways. The late Dolly Dowsett, Dunmow's local historian, remembered playing marbles and fivestones beside the pump. As late as 1908 Dunmow's water supply still depended on this and another town pump, together with various private wells.

Ford Bridge, Dunmow.

4. Down the Braintree road one could splash through the ford in the footsteps of Roman and Saxon, or cross over the River Chelmer more decorously by the bridge. When this card was sent about 1912 the writer made an interesting comment: 'There has been three or four accidents at Dunmow, and one well-known man in Dunmow had a sad accident against this bridge and died Wednesday morning. This is the ford bridge, down the Braintree road...' The Chelmer, rising in the region of Debden, could, in those days, cause considerable floods, when the ford was quite impassable and the bridge became a veritable lifeline. Today the ford can hardly be detected, the bridge has been widened, and the field beside it, with a footpath running through, has been officially designated as a picnic park, with the cricket field beyond.

Ford Bridge, Dunmow

Valentines Series

5. In this undated postcard, produced before 1920, we stand on the far side of the ford looking back towards Dunmow. The Ford Bridge takes the Braintree road across the Chelmer which is running very full after recent rain. A family sits on the opposite bank, no doubt eyeing the cameraman with that curiosity which in these early days was aroused by the unusual operations of the photographer in capturing a view for the production of a post-card. Until the advent of the town's bypass this bridge was a vital link between east and west, from Colchester to Bishops Stortford. Today the bridge has been rebuilt and the road widened, but the fields on either side retain the pleasant natural aspect. A new element in the view is the sight from the bridge of the traffic now flowing away from it on the Dunmow Bypass.

6. The history of these houses in the Avenue, back towards town off the Braintree road, is definitely known because Hasler and Clapham, the well-known local firm of millers, recorded in 1908 as corn and seed merchants and brick and tile manufacturers, decided, in that year, to develope for building purposes the land they owned on the corner of Braintree Road and Chelmsford Road, called White Post Pasture. It led to a quite separate development of two streets of houses, including the Avenue, where one of the houses is actually dated 1908. It was a successful speculation; within two years we see people as varied as the Reverend William Martin of the Primitive Methodists and Mr. Percy Robinson, commercial traveller, taking up residence here. The road looks very much the same today, though its pavements are now kerbed with little stone blocks which must have been laid soon after the houses were built and this photograph was taken.

High Street. South View. Dunmow.

7. This card is postmarked August, 1905. The view, from the south, shows on the left the signboard, unreadable, of the White Lion, a very old inn, but described at this time as: 'Family and commercial hotel; livery and bait stables; large billiard saloon; good accommodation for cyclists.' It was run by Douglas Bayly. Older Dunmow folk will remember that the Ancient Order of Foresters met there regularly. To the right we can see that the tradesmen's horses are being brought out from the stables behind the old White Hart, to be put into their carts prior to setting out on their delivery rounds. Beside the inn is the large shop of Charles E. Stokes, the butcher and purveyor who was still there at 73, High Street at least until the last war.

HIGH STREET, DUNMOW.

8. In our postcards we have come a little further along the High Street and have paused to look back. The road, after wet weather, looks very muddy, but the road sweeper has already made neat piles of horse dung and dirt in the gutter, ready for the cart to collect. Since it was in 1899 that stone paving was first proposed, and seeing that the pavement here looks so new and neat, this postcard must have appeared at the very beginning of the twentieth century. The buildings are identified in further views, but there is an odd feature here, for which no explanation has been forthcoming: a long string crosses the pavement from the fence in the left foreground and is tied to a stick in the middle of the road. A piece of white cloth is tied to it – perhaps as a warning to traffic – but why is it there?

9. The white house seen well down the road in the previous postcard is now seen in close-up with the men and the implements which constitute the business of Charles Julius Butcher, agricultural engineer and wheelwright – not to be confused with Charlie Butcher, the higgler and poulterer. The haymaking, reaping and other farm machines seen here show all the complications of horse-drawn agricultural equipment in the last years before motorisation. The house itself is dated 1885, high up under the eaves at the side; the photograph must have been taken some ten years later. In 1936 the house was dismantled, transported in pieces and re-erected on a site off the Stortford road.

10. Moving northwest along the High Street, and looking back the way we have come we see a wagon on its way from the brewery off Market Square passing, on the left, houses which today form the office of P.J. Rayner, builders' draughtsman and surveyor and then, with an extension on the end, the office and showroom of Colin Ivory cars. The magnificent chestnut tree, seen here in full bloom, has gone and so have the gates below it, leaving an access road to properties behind the car showrooms and the neighbouring Dunmow Inn. Across the road, under the other chestnut tree, can be seen the window of the White Lion inn. At the extreme right of the foreground the entrance to New Street can just be detected. The Cenotaph was to be sited here later.

DUNMOW 594.

Fred Spalding.
photo.
Chelmsford.
Copyright.

11. Moving just a little further on, in the steps of photographer Fred Spalding, we see on the right the mouth of New Street more clearly defined and beside it the old house, which we see today has been adapted as the offices of the Dunmow site of the Uttlesford District Council. Called the White House, it was at one time used as a convent. Around 1894 it was the home of Frederick Bartley, later the Livermores lived here. The birds against the sky look larger than life – and they are, for it was one of Fred Spalding's eccentricities to draw birds in on the negative where he felt that an expanse of sky needed some relief. The White Lion is now clearly seen beyond the chestnut tree on the right. Today it gives hospitality to an Indian restaurant, to Serendipity and to Video Spectacular, but the facia of the old inn can still be easily appreciated, though it is all now called Tudor Court.

12. The focal point of this postcard is the War Memorial, which helps to date the scene to shortly after the Great War, around 1920. The iron column on the other side of the street serves a more prosaic purpose as a vent for the sewerage system. To improve its effect on the landscape the top is finished in the shape of a crown. The shop with its blind down, on the left, is Dowsett's, remembered by older Dunmow folk for its marvellous collection of toys for sale. On the other side of the road, in the middle distance, the White Lion illustrates the march of time; it has turned from a coaching inn to a temperance hotel offering luncheons and teas. Right beside it stands a primitive petrol pump, sign that the times were indeed changing.

13. The memorial to 84 Dunmow men who gave their lives in the Great War stands white and pure. The date is 17th July 1921; the time, a Sunday afternoon; the place, the junction of New Street and High Street. General Byng, by this time Lord Byng of Vimy, has just unveiled the monument and the Union Jack has fallen away to the plinth, the buglers have sounded the last post and the Bishop of Chelmsford is at this moment gesturing in the course of his address of dedication. Soon the band, stationed in Mr. Floyd's garden to the left of the picture, will play the National Anthem and the soldiers will march away, the townsfolk will drift away, and the families affected will continue to mourn their losses.

Dunmow. New Street and Chapel.

14. From the memorial the photographer walked up New Street and turned around to take this view, with the Congregational Chapel on the righthand side. It was built by Cole Brothers in architect C. Pertwee's very decorative Romanesque style in 1869 when nonconformist religious enthusiasm was such that 955 seats were provided. It can be seen that, at this time, around 1900, the pavements were unpaved and un-kerbed but the lanterns on the walls of the houses show that the town was already lit by gas, supplied by the Dunmow Gas Company, under the chairmanship of Mr. W. De Vins Wade. New Street then was wholly residential, but people like Alfred King, the tailor, could work at home, and Tom King, insurance agent, probably made his books on the living-room table. By 1910 Ambrose Smith had set up here as watch and clock maker and the Staines, mother and daughter, made boots and dresses respectively.

15. Dunmow drowses in the morning sun early in the year around 1910. On the lefthand side, the house on the corner of New Street continued down to recent times as the office of A.E. Floyd, solicitor. Next come the premises of Stacey's, florist and photographer, who had glasshouses at the back, down the alleyway, on the other side of which Mr. Stock and his son Frank had their blacksmith's shop. The pillared portico marks the entrance to the Hazels, now the Dunmow Club. On the righthand side in the foreground we see Dowsett's newsagent's shop, where the board below the window advertises that parcels for the carrier Boyton and Turner can be left there. The gables of the old White Horse come next; the bracket sticks out from the wall, but the sign is missing. At this time William Ayton was the landlord.

16. Two men sitting in a wheelbarrow in the middle of Dunmow High Street would, today, be quite unbelievable. Back in 1900 however, it was just a pleasant prank in the noonday sun. On the lefthand side Mr. Floyd's house has a garden which has gone now, and its porch has been quite altered. Other houses on that side, for the most part, keep their outward appearance today. On the right, by the ancient, much-pollarded lime tree, the sign of the Boar's Head can just be made out. Thomas Harris was landlord, succeeded by his son Alfred who was still there in 1910; and the Boars's Head today offers refreshment in surroundings much like those our great grandfathers enjoyed.

17. This is another postcard produced by Spalding's of Chelmsford, family photographers spanning three generations and all called Fred. They operated for nearly a century from before 1860. The long shadows indicate that late on a day at the turn of the century Fred, the second generation and most ubiquitous photographer, came walking down Dunmow High Street looking for a view. The water carrier had just finished filling his tank – the trough he used to lead the water across still leans against the pump – and is probably glad to be finished with task of working the arm of that pump for such a long time. He would have eyed enviously the food and drink displayed in the window of William Adams, the provision dealer and wine and spirit merchant across the road. By 1906 Adams' son Richard Henry had taken over. Now the site is occupied by Fred. J. Staines shoe shop, the Anglia Building Society and Cook's the wine merchants.

18. We see the High Street from the northwest as photographed by Fred Spalding around 1905. The first shop on the left is Henry Knight's the watchmaker. On the right Mrs. Johnson and her son William offer all that is best in drapery and millinery, performing at the same time all the functions of the Post Office, including the halfpenny (one fifth of the present penny) stamp for this card. The curving bracket above the shop has lost the lamp which was still in use in 1902 as shown in other photographs. The darker stain in the gutter on the left shows where the wasted water has run from the pump; proof of its continued importance in the life of the town's main street. The alleyway on the right is Angel Lane, leading still, today, to the Baptist church.

19. Arthur Archer is shown in 1910 County Directory as a cycle manufacturer and agent. His windows show clearly just how very many brands of English cycles and accessories he could offer. That he had been there some time is shown by the missing letters on the advertisements. He had purchased this property in the High Street before 1900; this photograph was taken a few years later but well before 1930, when the firm was re-titled A. Archer and Sons. The car seen here was the first to be owned by a Dunmow resident, a Mr. Hodges. The shop as shown here is now Butcher and Son Electrical Ltd. Beside is the entrance to the town's car park. The wall of the Boar's Head on the other side just appears to the right.

20. One of the rare views taken by Henry Bradley, Dunmow's tailor and outfitter, who was a keen amateur photographer. This postcard, produced from a glass negative, is one of eight rescued from oblivion by Mr. L. Byford. On the lefthand side we just perceive Arthur Dennis's ironmongery, built in 1901 when some old cottages were demolished. Next to it a sign announces the public telephone available in the Post Office there. During the last war it was taken over as a British restaurant. Later it became a secondhand shop run by Oxfam and after that a dress shop. Then comes Roper's the chemist and Lloyd's Bank, which only recently had been Snow's the confectionery and toy shop. The white house next to it is the White Horse, standing on the side of a house run as an 'outlier' of Tilty Abbey. Today it is an Indian restaurant.

HIGH STREET, DUNMOW.

21. The garden rollers at the pavement's edge on the lefthand side have been put on view by Arthur Dennis, ironmonger, but the camera looks past his shop to the bow window of Roper's pharmacy, run at this time, about 1910, by Mr. J.H. Hole. Past the lamp-post on the left is the White Horse, just beyond that is Wood's the taylors. He started his business on Star Hill but by 1901 the directory shows him as 'Wood, Alfred William, tailor and breeches maker, High Street'. His business did not close until 1958, and many older people recall seeing the tailors in the window, sitting cross-legged, stitching away. On the righthand side Henry Bradley proudly stands in his shop entrance. He was owner, too, of the bootmakers' next door, where we see the telegraph messenger-boy with his bicycle clips on, ready for urgent action.

22. Henry Bradley was a man with a flair for business. He used his interest in photography, purely as an amateur, to produce this unusual postcard as an advertisement, in which his own portrait takes the central position. Surrounding it are his own photographs of, from the top and reading clock-wise, Doctor's Pond, the Congregational Church in New Street, the Town Hall, his own shops in the High Street and the parish church. It would seem that he took over the tailors, outfitters and boot and shoe manufacturers business from Charles Brand at the turn of the century, when Brand retired to Brick Kilns Farm. The business was carried on into recent times by Bradley's three daughters, one of whom, Miss M. Bradley, continued his interest in photography, supplying the illustrations for Frederick Robus's 'Dunmow and its Charters', published in 1923.

23. Arthur Willett proudly, almost brashly, shows his wares and his services around 1913. In 1937 he was still claiming to be, 'newsagent and wholesale distributor, stationer, musical instrument dealer, printing agent, tobacconist and umbrella maker', at 6, High Street. He and, or, his father started before the beginning of the century as a hairdresser in North Street. That they were well-established in the town is shown by the advertisement in the Essex Weekly News of Friday, 4th September, 1908: 'NOW READY, set of 12 beautiful colored, glossy, platesunk Postcards of the district, 1d. each. Set in Album, post free for 1s. 2d. – A. Willett, High Street, Dunmow.' It is pleasing to note that the shop continues, almost unaltered, to serve the present needs of the townsfolk.

24. The condition of the road at the junction of High Street and the Market Place shows that traffic is still horse-drawn, though the draincover is evidence of modern improvement. From this fact and the knowledge that flagstones for the pavement were introduced just after 1899, it would be reasonable to date this photograph to around 1910. By then J.G. Line's shop, on the corner, had changed from a confectioner's in 1894, to a pork butcher's and poulterer's run by Mrs. Fanny Line. Past the lamp-post on the left is Roper's, chemist, then the Snow's fancy goods repository. The last shop visible on the left is Carter's the stationer, printer and bookseller. A poem about Dunmow, on paper watermarked 1839, includes: *The printing press, if I forget, Tis clear I shall be wrong, And Carter very likely say, He will not print the song,* proving Carter's long establishment in the town.

DUNMOW TOWN HALL

25. On a summer's morning around 1909 we see, on the right, the butcher's and poulterer's, J.G. Line. 'The International Tea Co.'s Stores Limited, grocers and tea dealers' is entered in the 1910 directory of Essex. Between the two stands the unusual Town Hall, now in private hands. It is thought to have been built originally between 1560 and 1570 but it was enlarged and partly rebuilt in the nineteenth century. Dunmow was established as a Borough as early as 1555, confirmed by Queen Elizabeth in 1590, but it was too small to qualify as a borough under the act of 1885, so it lost that status, though it did become the headquarters of the Dunmow Rural District Council which was itself absorbed into the larger Uttlesford District Council in 1974. The old Town Hall shows striking differences in its outward appearance today, from the entrance to the oversailing of the upper storey and the treatment of the large window.

26. The Dunmow Town Band is striking up the National Anthem and the men in the crowd are just beginning to take off their hats. The townspeople have assembled to celebrate the diamond jubilee of Queen Victoria's reign on 20th June 1897. In 'Dunmow Through the Ages' Dorothy Dowsett writes: 'For Queen Victoria's diamond jubilee celebrations Dunmow looked gayer than anyone could remember having seen it on previous celebrations, even the golden jubilee. The decorations were profuse and artistic. If any house should be singled out for individual mention it would be that of Dr. Lyle. At midday the Market Place was thronged with the inhabitants who had been asked to meet there to join in the singing of the National Anthem... Sports took place in the afternoon... The rejoicings concluded with a monster torchlight procession and bonfire...'

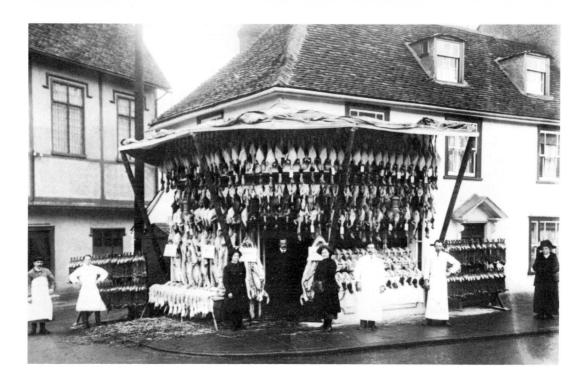

27. Charles H. Stokes has taken over Line's shop on the corner of the High Street and Market Place, next to the Town Hall, which can be seen on the left. Stokes' name cannot be seen, though enough of it can be divined with a magnifying glass, because the shop front is completely hidden by this very decorative stall to display some of the entries and the award-winners in the Dunmow Fatstock Show. The appearance of the telegraph pole to the left of the display and the two white insulators carrying the wires further left on the wall of the Town Hall puts the date of this postcard between 1905 and 1910. It was in 1905 that the Dunmow District Agriculture Competitions Association revived shows like this to encourage healthy competition and keep the old standards. Prizes were offered for the best thatching, stacking and hedging, and there were classes for all kinds of produce.

Fred Spalding
photo
Chelmsford Copyright

MARKET SQUARE DUNMOW 461

28. Fred Spalding (1858-1947), the well-known Chelmsford photographer, walked a little way up the Stortford Road, then turned and took this photograph to add to his extensive stock of postcards of Essex scenes. No telephone poles or wires obstruct the view, so it can be dated earlier than the previous view, probably around 1900. While Line's, the butchers, looks closed, Dennis the ironmonger has the usual display of wheelbarrows and water carts on the pavement. As to the Town Hall, the 1894 County Directory tells us: 'The Town Hall, standing in the centre of the town, was built in 1578, repaired in 1760 and enlarged in 1837 and 1855, and in 1888 it was purchased by the principal inhabitants for the benefit of the town.'

29. Now we proceed with those early photographers up the Stortford Road. The interesting corner doorway to R. Gillham & Son, butchers, who bought the business about 1900, remains unaltered to this day. The butcher holds his knife in readiness, as if he were about to cut up the whole sheep hanging there. Next door, where the cheeky errand boy leans against the shuttered window, is Arthur J. Barham, watchmaker and jeweller. The last house visible on the left is the Chequers Inn. It was trading under that sign at least as early as 1826 when William Smith was the landlord. Gillham's is now Metson and Down, travel and insurance agents, and they have taken over the whole floor of the house. The next house has had a door and a set of steps removed; then Forge Cottages stand sadly empty. Above them a Chinese take-away, the Happy Garden, is now in business.

30. The horse has been dared to move while the photographer focusses his camera! It is a smart trap that the butcher's boy takes on his delivery round – even the horses hooves are polished. 'T. LUCKIN' appears on the shop front, but Mrs. Jane Luckin was already a widow by 1894 and was running the business herself. It is in Stortford Road and, happily, the interesting shop front continues practically unaltered and is still a butcher's – J.G. Sweetland. A copy of this photograph is displayed in the window on the spotless slab, together with horse brasses awarded as prizes in the Dunmow Horse and Cart Parade prior to the Great War. It is more than likely that the horse and trap photographed was a successful entry.

31. At one time in its long history the Royal Oak, off the Stortford Road, is said to have been called the Flitch of Bacon. By 1910, the likely date of this postcard, James Nelson was running it. He has been described as a 'regular quick-wit' who challenged the socialists, led by the Reverend Maxted, when they came to preach their creed in Market Square. Kemp, smart and sophisticated, stands at his gate. The polished brassplate on the porch proclaims 'J.N. Kemp wine and spirits merchant'. The windows sparkle in their cleanliness. Beneath one is the rather unsusual notice announcing that the Encyclopaedia Britannica may be consulted within. The only incongruous note is struck by the election poster stuck on the chimney stack.

32. The Queen Victoria, off the Stortford Road at Threaders Green, a small hamlet, is a popular place today with the right atmosphere for the regular gathering of young farmers. This postcard is dated 27th August 1915, when the place was more an alehouse than an inn. It would have served the carter and the waggoner, the farmer and his men with their pint of ale and bread and cheese when it first began as the front room of a cottage. On the sunny morning shown here the carter is taking his mid-morning break, having given his horse the nose-bag which contains its meal. The bicycles to be seen emphasise the scattered nature of the houses here and the distance from town; the young mother adjusting the pram canopy has to push the baby and the toddler sitting on the end of the pram quite a distance to do her shopping.

33. Another view of the Queen Victoria shows two early tourists admiring the beerhouse and its setting around 1905. The lady on the left could be carrying one of the latest pocket-sized cameras. The 'Tap' indicates that the beer was brewed on the premises and could be drawn by tap straight from the large barrel or vat. The old cottage in the background still looks today as it does in this picture, having been recently re-thatched. The ornate signpost has been replaced, with wrought-iron scroll work carrying on the old tradition, but necessary modern alterations include the broad car park beside the restaurant extension, the council houses round the green across the road and the busy road itself – no place today for free-ranging chicken.

34. Here we reach the extent of our journey through Dunmow and up the Stortford Road. By 1912, date of this postcard, the number of bars on the telegraph pole shows the rapid spread of the service and already modern houses have been built to take advantage of the situation up on the hill in clean air with wonderful views. In those days the railway was part of the view as trains puffed along the line just below the Queen Victoria; now road traffic thunders along the Dunmow bypass, using the line of the old railway.

35. With the photographer returning down the Stortford Road we see the Royal Oak on the right. The postcard was actually posted in 1915; more and more tourists are taking to their bicycles and so the enterprising landlord has added to his sign 'Good accommodation for cyclists'. Down the road, beneath the trees, one of the new motor cars and a motor cycle shatter the drowsy silence of sunny Dunmow with the noise of their 'infernal', internal combustion engines. The Three Tuns, closed these many years, is here still hanging out its sign. The beauty of its splendid old doorway can still be appreciated today. To the far right, from its own bracket beneath the Royal Oak's signboard there is suspended, just like the trade symbols of medieval times, one of the old stone jars in which the brewery supplied its ale.

Stortford Road.

36. Smoke from the chimney curls upward to show that the Three Tuns is still very much lived in, and the faded sign shows that the inn has been refreshing travellers through many years. It was closed even before the last war, though the bracket from which that old signboard swung is still in position. At one time there was a candle factory behind the inn, owned and run by the landlord, John George Mackenzie. He had led the Three Tuns to Alfred Low in the eighteen-nineties, while he, himself, acted as the town's assistant overseer and tax collector. In the first house shown on this postcard, produced about 1912, lived Walter Ketley, the local builder and plasterer, who named his four daughters Faith, Hope, Charity and Mercy. Beyond the houses, the chestnut trees, here in glorious bloom, stand on the site of the present Smith's Garage. Some of the trees on the right still exist in front of the present fire station.

Fred Spalding, Photo. Chelmsford. Copyright.

STORTFORD ROAD, DUNMOW. 465.

37. A little further towards the town centre, at the beginning of the Stortford Road, we see on the left the chestnut trees which still burgeon in the grounds of The Chestnuts, a large house now acting as the registered offices of so many companies that it has more brass plates than any other building in Dunmow. At this time, around 1900, J.G. Lines, the butchers, straight ahead on the corner of High Street and Market Square, was still in business, though run by his widow, Fanny. She was in competition with R. Gillham and Son, the butchers seen on the right of the photograph, next the alleyway called Taylor's Piece today. The shop front stands unaltered, but it is now Metson and Down, the travel and insurance agents.

38. Back in the High Street at the junction with Market Square Fred Spalding focussed his camera towards the Star Inn. He must have come here just after 1906, when F. Sewell and Company, general drapers, occupied the shop on the lefthand side. It is now Jeeves. The International Stores were at this time quite a newcomer, their first entry in the County Directory under Dunmow can be traced to 1906 when they are shown as 'International Tea Co.'s Store Limited, grocers and tea dealers, Market Place'. Pannell's, immediately below them, under its four gables, has a big flagpole, a landmark down to recent times, but it differs from the next postcard in that the bold, gilt lettering has not yet been affixed across its façade.

39. After the last view we see the Town Hall in rather a dilapidated state. Plaster peeling from the walls exposes the lath-and-plaster construction beneath, proving original building in the sixteenth century. T.W. Pannell's, fruiterer and fishmonger, have, since the previous photograph was taken, erected a sign all across their facia which proudly points to their establishment in 1891; perhaps it was a reaction to the competition from, and the brass edging to the International Stores on which its name was proclaimed in large letters. A difference can also be detected in the street lamp attached to the wall of the Town Hall; since the previous postcard it appears to have been converted from gas to electricity. Below Pannell's is Savill's, a sadler and harnessmaker in Victorian times, owned by Frederick Savill. He handed it on to his son Leubert G. Savill who was still there up to the Great War, the approximate date of this postcard. Now it is a wool shop.

40. This postcard was one of a series taken by Fred Spalding about 1910. With the heavy equipment required for photography in those days Mr. Spalding, who would have had to drive over from the Chelmsford shop in his horse and trap, would have taken as many views as possible in one day, to save further journeys. He stood down by the Star to take this scene, showing the side of Market Square known as Rood End, reference to the old market cross. On the far right is Luckin's the grocers, being run by Samuel at this time and still trading under that name today. Next to them is F. Lewis, ironmongers and oil merchants who, new to the town, believed in the principle of shouting one's wares. They wrote 'Lewis for everything' all across their front and spread their goods out temptingly across the pavement.

41. Fred Spalding was standing with his back to this building when he took the photograph for the preceding postcard. It is the Star Inn, seen here on, or very close to 9th August 1902, the day of the coronation of King Edward VII. 'E.R.' is worked in coloured lights between the bedroom windows and they will blaze out dramatically at night. Flags, banners and a crown above the door are daytime decoration. Proof of the date is the poster on the right which advertises the Bishops Stortford Flower Show to be held on 13th August 1902. Over the door can be detected the name of the licencee, William Turner. He had taken over from James Jordan and by 1906 had himself been succeeded by Frank Springham.

Doctors' Pond. Dunmow

42. Doctor's Pond, below the Star, looks very tranquil in this postcard, sent in August 1907. The pond was there long before Dr. Raynor became associated with it at the end of the eighteenth century. He took a great interest in it, even stocked it with fish. Our point of view is from the west end with the Downs behind us. Alexia Wilson, in her 'A Dunmow Diary', of 1951, rhymes amusingly: *Take a glance at the pond,/ The gossips declare/ The waste from the beer/ Goes into the pond/ But that is all rubbish, 'tis surely the pond/ That makes us such tasty and beautiful beer.* The reference is to the Dunmow Brewery, on the other side of the road, next to the King's Head. In this view the orchard and the wall have gone and two houses have taken their place.

43. On 22nd July 1930 a member of the Historical Association, at Dunmow for a meeting, sent this card off to a friend. The origin of the pond, seen here from the east end, has never been ascertained. Dorothy Dowsett has said: 'If one stops to think, with three hills and springs running down it was quite likely a natural pond. Alternatively it was dug out by man to save flooding, and this long before Dr. Raynor stocked it with fish.' The Directory of 1792 shows John Raynor as a surgeon and apothecary. The pond was used for a very practical purpose when Lionel Lukin, born here in 1742, tried out the first self-righting lifeboat which he had invented in 1785.

44. Brook House, which stands in busy North Street, exactly opposite Rosemary Lane, was built in the fifteenth century. Its condition here shows later additions, such as the verandah, of Victorian origin, which with the wheel of fashion, have then been removed. The large-scale Ordnance Survey map of 1897 shows the brook after which it was named still running under the road some twenty-seven yards to the north. In the last decade of the nineteenth century Miss Wade resided at Brook House. By 1905 William Scarfe was living there, conveniently close to the British School of which he was master. The school was built in 1844 right beside Doctor's Pond.

45. Standing at the front gate of Brook House in 1904 we look, on the left hand, up North Street where the chimneys of the Dunmow and Crown breweries rise against the sky. In the centre of the picture two boys pose for the camera in front of a huge mound of gravel which has only just been dumped there for the purpose of making up Rosemary Lane, running up the hill on the right, which up to this date was hardly more than a muddy track. Downs House, on the corner between the two roads, looks very much the same today – perhaps even more shrouded in greenery. The fencing shown here along the verge of Rosemary Lane is not there today and the lamp-post, which here looks out of commission, has been removed altogether.

DUNMOW.—ROSEMARY LANE

46. This is the upper part of Rosemary Lane, just before it joins the Stortford Road. Since it is properly surfaced it would appear to have been photographed shortly after 1906, the date of the previous postcard. The street lamps seem to be giving trouble; the one in the foreground does not look complete and up by the junction a man perched on a ladder is working on another one. It was in 1906 that the gas lamps were altered from the flare type to the incandescent type which used a 'mantle' to contain the flame. The gas company undertook to provide fifty-five such lamps and to light them from August to May for an annual sum of £125. In earlier days Rosemary Lane was known as Windmill Street, but the date of, and reason for the change cannot now be ascertained.

Dunmow. Rosemary Lane.

Stacey, Dunmow.

47. The date on this postcard is 8th June 1905. It gives a intriguing view of Rosemary Lane, not so much because of the free-ranging pig seen in the right foreground, but because of the groups of men further up the lane. They appear to be standing stiffly to attention, or pausing for the photographer in the process of marching. Four of the men look as though they are drummers. It could be a postcard left over from the celebrations of the coronation of Edward VII in August 1902. In the 1890's William Stacey was a nurseryman and photographer. His son Reginald concentrated on the photography side and established his shop in the High Street, where Stacey's is still serving the public as a high-class greengrocer. Today both the wall and the hedge in the foreground of this photograph is no longer there.

48. The Downs occupies an area between Doctor's Pond and Buildings Farm across Rosemary Lane. When the visitor sent this card on 6th May 1909 the Downs were dreaming in warm sunshine; even the ducks are drowsy. From the Downs we are looking south over the roofs and gardens of the houses which lie behind the Star Inn, between Star Hill and Star Lane. The chimneys of the Crown Brewery act as a landmark on the horizon. This view is from the north side of the Pond. The bungalow on the right was demolished and two houses now stand on the land covered by it and the adjoining orchard, but in general the roof lines are very similar today. It is quite evident to any Sunday morning visitor that feeding the ducks has retained its popularity through the generations.

THE DOWNS AND DOCTOR'S POND, DUNMOW

49. We are looking eastward across the Doctor's Pond from Rosemary Lane in 1930 or a little earlier. This is the area of greenery from the pond back to the other side of Rosemary Lane which is known locally as the Downs. The pond looks very peaceful, but there have been some high old times around it and in it. For example, many an entrant got a wetting when they tried to negotiate the greasy pole cantilevered out across it during the celebrations of Queen Victoria's diamond jubilee in 1897. Ten years earlier, to celebrate the golden jubilee, similar fun and games had been arranged for the children of the National School right beside the Pond. It is plain to see today that Doctor's Pond has a special place in the affections of the townspeople.

67682. THE DOWNS. GREAT DUNMOW.

50. Long shadows from east to west and the sight of the milk cart on its way indicate that this is an early morning photograph. The churns are lodged at the front of the cart. The milkman, who in those days was often the same man who milked the cows on the local farm, used a dipper of regulation size to fill the housewife's own jug. We are viewing the Downs, still preserved as an open space, from the road leading to Buildings Farm. Doctor's Pond lies behind the trees in the background. This postcard, kept as a souvenir, was never sent, so there is no postmark to help us in the dating. From the look of the motorcycle and sidecar and from the registration number, F 6085, we can ascribe it to the early 1920's. The scene is much the same today, though the further house has had a gable inserted and its verandah altered.

51. We follow the photographer to the Causeway. The house in the foreground is known today as 'The Limes'. Its modern rendering hides sixteenth-century construction. As to the story of the house just beyond it, 'Clock House, we see from the church register that William Beaumont, of Clock House, younger brother of the late Vicar Thomas Beaumont', was buried in 1729. Thomas Beaumont was Vicar here from 1678 to 1710. In 1848 the house is shown in the directory as 'Clock House Diocesan School'. It is thought to have been built in the late sixteenth century, making it the oldest brick house in Dunmow. Its mullioned windows and its Dutch-style gables are original; even some of the glass is contemporary. The central, white-painted, timber turret houses a clock which is said to be a replica of that on Dover Castle. In the cupola above hangs a bell founded by Bryan Eldridge in 1651. Today it is a private house, not open to visitors.

52. The Harp, in the hands of John Bush, was dispensing ale to thirsty townsfolk at Church end long before its entry in the 1826 directory. A local survey of weights and measures in 1756 shows James Wilson as the licensed victualler. It is not certain just when the Harp, as it were, took up its Angel. Fred Spalding had taken this photograph by 1910 and reproduced it for sale around the county as one of his famous series of postcards. Today the pub's central lantern has gone, but two smaller ones flank the door, and all the greenery has had to go in the interest of car parking. Another change is on the left of the postcard, where today a new house shows its blank side between the old house and the church tower.

53. It is nearly half past two on a sunny day around 1908. At the time the County Directory was telling people: 'The church of St. Mary the Virgin is a large and ancient building of stone in the Decorated and Perpendicular styles... and an embattled west tower with angle turrets containing a clock and 6 bells...' Nikolaus Pevsner, the expert on old buildings, describes St. Mary's as: '...Pebble-rubble and externally all of a piece, although, alas, all very restored...' Perhaps it is to the credit of the parishioners of Dunmow that their church has been restored and kept in good order through more than five hundred years. At this time the Vicar was the Reverend John Evans. One local worshipper remembers: 'He came to us with very high recommendations, which were fully appreciated here. He was very popular with all classes.'

2252 ST MARY'S CHURCH, DUNMOW.

54. The east window of St. Mary the Virgin is, according to the experts, 'unusually sumptuous'. It has five 'lights', or areas of glass framed in stone. Here we see it as it looked around 1915. Because the people of Dunmow have kept their church in good order all down the years, postcards like this are almost impossible to date if they have not been through the post. This view shows the church in what might be termed its original state. In the church itself one can see a change in that one of the south aisle windows contains fragments of fifteenth-century glass which have been re-assembled in a fascinating kaleidoscope of colour. The aisle windows have all been renewed. The south porch, visible at the extreme left, is notable for its priest's room, of the late fifteenth century, which is extended into the church itself as a gallery.

ST. MARY'S CHURCH, DUNMOW

55. We have seen that Vicar Evans was highly thought of during his ten years incumbency from 1905. His portrait is inset on this postcard, dating it to about 1910. The medieval sedilia (seats for the priests) and the piscina (basin for washing the holy utensils of communion) were revealed in 1855 when women were scraping plaster from the walls. The present pews are the result of a thorough-going restoration in 1872-73 after the Reverend W.L. Scott had declared: 'The state of Dunmow church is a reproach to us... The old and ugly pews still hold their place in the main part of the church and are becoming every day meaner and shabbier; the coarse brick pavement more worn and uneven...' The pews went, so did the galleries and the church took on the open aspect which allowed the architecture, particularly the grand tower arch, to be fully enjoyed.

Dunmow.

56. A serene view of the Church of St. Mary the Virgin. A sad note is introduced by the view of the recent graves in the foreground, still covered with floral tributes. The bowler-hatted man, possibly the verger, has taken off his jacket and rolled up his sleeves to help the sexton complete an interment. The tower is one of the finest features of the church, rising almost eighty feet to the very tip of the corner turrets. The peal of eight bells is reckoned by campanologists to be one of the best in the county. Six of the bells are dated to particular years in the seventeenth century, one is undated, and the other two were added in 1927. That would be about seven years after the production of this postcard.

57. We leave Church End, heading across the river up the Stebbing Road. A smiling young lady of fashion poses for Fred Spalding in the summer of 1900, standing on the bridge which was rebuilt and re-opened on 7th June 1882. The Reverend Langston Scott gives us an eyewitness account of the event: 'The weather was brilliant and the whole place presented a real gala appearance… Everyone was delighted to welcome Lord and Lady Brooke on this their first appearance among us since their marriage a year ago.' The band of the 2nd. Essex Rifle Volunteers played manfully, Lady Brooke, better known later as Countess Warwick, formally laid the last stone in the presence of some three thousand inhabitants.

58. Crouches Farm still gets a mention on the Ordnance Survey maps. It lies on the righthand side of the Stebbing Road after crossing the bridge at Church End seen in the previous postcard. Back in 1803 the valuation of the place was put at £74.10s.0d. with the farmer, Mr. J. Scruby, senior, having to pay yearly tithes of nearly nineteen pounds. In 1894 John William Barnard was the tenant, but by 1906 Percy Wallis is shown there as a private resident rather than as a farmer, and he was still there in 1910, the probable date of issue of this postcard. The barn is seen on the right, the house lies behind the trees above the horse and trap. Today the view is just as rural all round, though the older trees have been removed, the barn has been dismantled, and the old, lean-on-me, five-barred gate has been replaced by the colder, more practical welded-metal kind.

59. The country lane, albeit the main road to Thaxted, now classified as the A130, is still very primitively surfaced. An equally primitive drain opens at the edge of the unkerbed verge, but deep puddles have formed in the roadside ditch. Street lighting, seen on this site in the next postcard, has not yet been provided. Being on the edge of town, just up Beaumont Hill beyond the Causeway, this is not surprising. In the thatched cottage on the left lived Mr. George Ellis, carter and small farmer who, by 1906, was succeeded by his son Harry. It now has a modern extension. When Henry Bradley came along in 1912 to add this view to his collection, the house in the foreground was already hundreds of years old. Since the date of this postcard it was allowed to deteriorate until it fell down and was replaced by the present house.

Parsonage Down Hill, Dunmow.

60. Having seen the previous postcard we can now note the transformation, for this is claimed to be the first road in Dunmow to be made of poured, reinforced concrete. It was made, as was the postcard, just before the First World War. It was later called Beaumont Hill, honouring the Beaumont family of Clock House, just down the road and round the bend. Their connection with the town goes all the way back to the man who was Vicar here in 1678. The gas lamp, of functional yet dignified design, is a recent extension of the town's original lighting by gas which started as early as 1846. Rainwater still drained into open ditches, as seen beside the footpath on the left. Today the road is uniformly metalled throughout and the early concrete is concealed.

Parsonage Hill.

61. Once again, in 1912 or thereabouts, Henry Bradley recorded a moment in the story of Dunmow – and a strange little happening. Under a magnifying glass it can be seen that the woman in the road is carrying the head and foot of an iron bedstead, while her companion on the footpath carries the connecting pieces. In those days such a bedstead was a prized object, handed down in the family. But for this little cameo of the past, the view today is almost exactly the same from halfway up Parsonage Hill, or Beaumont Hill as it was later called, though the road is now kerbed. Mr. Archer lived in one of the further cottages and Mrs. Sadler in the nearer, which today has been extended and is called Stormy Cottage. A white picket fence has replaced the rambling hedge.

Dunmow.

62. At the top of Beaumont Hill on the Thaxted road the cottages look across to a little pool in a hollow, known locally as Cricketer's Pond after the public house on the other side of the road. At the time of this postcard, around 1910, James Clarke was the landlord and the local baker, selling his bread and confectionery in the shop with the blind down which is still an integral part of the Cricketers and a shop no longer. The pond was a favourite playing place for the children round about. The view today is much the same, though the pond has shrunk considerably and its banks are now overgrown with young trees and undergrowth. The thatched cottage at the extreme left has been replaced with a modern house and the tree beside it has gone in the interest of providing an extended car park for the Cricketers.

63. A view across the Cricketers Pond taken by Fred Spalding about 1910 shows the Cricketers being given a thorough redecoration, although business appears to continue in the baker's shop which is part of it. It may be that the wall of the shop front was lowered at this time, down to the threshold level, to give a larger, more modern window to tempt in the customers. James Clarke was baker and beer retailer at this time. The wagonette is waiting for the lady seen through the shop doorway. Today the sign has been moved down the road just a little and the pub car park spreads out beside it on the lefthand side where at this time there was a cottage garden. The cottage behind the hedge on the far left has been replaced by a modern dwelling.

DUNMOW.—BOWYER'S BRIDGE

64. Richard Bowyer is mentioned in 1489 in the national 'Ministers' Accounts' kept in the Public Record Office. It is assumed that the bridge named after him was built to his order originally to carry the Thaxted road across the Chelmer below Elmbridge Mill. On the large-scale map of 1897 it can be seen that there was little to choose between what we call the main road and that which goes to Thaxted via Little Easton. In fact, the present A130 was a turning off the main road at this point. Bowyers Bridge Cottage as it is now called is the house seen on the postcard, but today it has been altered and extended out of all recognition. The road and the bridge have been widened and realigned and those fine old trees have met their fate in the process.

High Street Little Dunmow

65. At Little Dunmow the lorry and the electricity cables help to date this postcard to the late 1920's. Buildings then were still showing the natural, local materials used in their construction – thatch from reeds by the river, wattle and daub from hazel copses and Essex clay, tiles from the brick earth found in the clay and clapboard from the trees which grew all around. Every building in this picture is the same today, except for two windows added to the front and side of the little extension on the clapboard house. By the lorry the Flitch of Bacon public house presents its eighteenth-century windows to the world. It was run by Frederick Hockley from as early as 1910 and then by his widow Alice down to the Second World War. Its sign perpetuates the ancient custom of giving a flitch, or side of bacon to a couple who could, on oath, swear that they had lived in perfect harmony and not repented their marriage for a year and a day.

Priory Cottages · Little Dunmow   67712

66. The Priory Cottages, Little Dunmow, subject of this postcard of about 1920, remind us of the famous priory founded here in 1104, according to David Coller, writing in 1861, who continues: 'The buildings have long since been razed. The walks and grounds, where the friars paced to and fro muttering their offices, are now corn fields. That quiet row of cottages, formerly a farmhouse, representing the dignity of the Priory Manor, stands on the site of the buildings within which the guest was welcomed and the feast was spread on saints' days and high festival.' The cottages grew more shabby and were practically falling down in the 1960's when Mr. Wilson bought them and had them thoroughly restored as the one house they were originally – a twelfth-century hall house of very unusual timber construction.

67. The old house in Grange Lane, Little Dunmow, seen in 1922. Once of great importance as the seat of the local ruling family in Elizabethan times, it descended to the status of a farmhouse, with a fine, thatched cart lodge which can be seen to the left of the postcard. By 1906 the agricultural depression had hit Essex so hard that amalgamations were inevitable. Grange Farm was then being held and worked in conjunction with Brook End, Bourchiers, Bayles and Rookwoods by the Metsons. The house had been converted to cottages for farm workers. Here the continuing dilapidations can be seen. It appears that the cottage nearest the camera is unoccupied. Today that section has completely disappeared and the whole building, now called Monks Hall, has reverted to one large private house. It now includes the two gabled sections and the centre section where the roof still sweeps down low; a sympathetic and attractive restoration.

Little Dunmow Church
ESSEX

NORRIS
PHOTO

68. One little girl, all alone, looks dwarfed by the wall of the church of St. Mary the Virgin at Little Dunmow. The postcard produced about 1920 shows the church in very good repair. It is the last surviving part of the Augustinian priory founded here in 1104 – just a small portion of the priory's original church; except, that is, for the slim tower built by James Brown, a Braintree man, in 1872, and called by Nikolaus Pevsner, the architectural expert, 'a silly turret'. Today's church, the Lady Chapel of the old Priory Church, survived because the villagers had used it from the earliest days as their particular place of worship. The view of the church today is identical, though now, unfortunately, it has to be kept locked, but the key can be obtained locally, as shown on the door.

Little Dunmow Church.

69. The interior of St. Mary's, Little Dunmow, is light and airy, thanks to the grand fourteenth-century nave windows and the modern east window. That this postcard was produced for sale in the 1920's is obvious from the touching memorial to villagers who fell in the First World War, partly visible in the first archway on the left, between the two candles. It was designed by Florence Burnett and carried out by W. Perry Leach and Sons of Cambridge. Sadly, the plaster has crumbled so badly that half the design is now missing, but it is moving to see that the flowers which adorn the memorial are constantly renewed. Just discernible on the postcard, to the left behind the pulpit are the arms of the famous 'Flitch' chair.

70. The fact that a photograph of an old chair knocked up from secondhand timber would be sold to tourists is a clear indication of that chair's significance. It is so very old, and was taken so much for granted by the villagers themselves that its true history has not been recorded. The timber in it has been dated to the thirteenth century, when it started life in the Priory Church as the end of a row of priors' stalls. Holes were made below the seat and long shafts passed through so that successful claimants of the flitch of bacon could be carried around the village in joyful celebration. It has been considered important enough to be included in the 1930 exhibition of English medieval art at the Victoria and Albert Museum.

71. It was a tradition in Great Dunmow that there should be the Horse-and-Cart Parade on Whit Monday with the town band in attendance, followed by fun and games. The sport included climbing the greasy pole slung out over Doctor's Pond. This postcard remembers the day in 1908, when just about everybody who was anybody paraded down the High Street, following the band and the beautifully turned out horse-drawn vehicles. The strong breeze which is tossing the blossom on the chestnut trees has also wrapped the great flag hoisted above the White Lion completely round its pole. The shop immediately on the left is E.J. Dowsett, the newsagent, who could have sold this and other, coloured postcards specially produced by Arthur Willett, another newsagent further along the High Street.

72. Could Dunmow ever have witnessed a busier scene than this? It is the occasion of the Horse and Cart Parade on Whit Monday in 1907 as proved by the postmark on the card. The judges of the smartest turn-out are using a cart (the shafts can be seen pointing upwards) as a viewing platform in front of the Saracen's Head. It was a popular site in those days for all kinds of presentation and public address, including awards for the ploughing match and the hedging, stacking and thatching competitions. The importance of agriculture in the area at this time is shown by the fact there there were at least twenty-one farmers listed in the immediate vicinity of the town, including the Barnards: Dan, Henry, Oswald and Thomas of Marks, Bigods, Roughie and Lower Hall farms respectively.

73. The Dunmow Pageant of 1912 can still be remembered by older folk as one of the greatest events ever staged in the town. It drew thousands of spectators and involved over three hundred townspeople in acting out the chapters in the Dunmow story, including the Flitch Ceremony of 1751, in suitable costume. Here we see the jury selected to judge the case of the claimants to a flitch. Mr. T. Gibbons who always 'examined for the bacon', was well-known for his humorous repartee. It was due to the famous novelist William Harrison Ainsworth that the Flitch Ceremony was revived not at Little, but at Great Dunmow on 19th July 1855. On that day some seven thousand people attended, special trains were laid on to Bishops Stortford from whence a convoy of horse-drawn vehicles carried the excited crowds to the Town Hall and then to Windmill Field, on the Downs, to see the spectacle.

74. After the grand re-introduction of the Flitch Trial, it was re-enacted intermittently down to 1890. In that year a very determined local committee kept the custom alive through to 1912. This was probably the best year of all, for the ceremony was included as part of the pageant of Dunmow history arranged by Hugh Cranmer-Byng, well-known local poet and writer. The scene shown here represents the chairing of a successful couple who claimed the flitch at the trial of 1751, one of the rare occasions in the eighteenth century when the ceremony was actually performed at Little Dunmow. The flitch is being carried before them on a long pole exactly as it was arranged in the ancient rules of the ceremony.

Dunmow Pageant 1751. Section No 2.

75. One could be forgiven for thinking that the camera had been invented by 1751, when Thomas Shakeshaft of Wethersfield, weaver, and Ann his wife were being chaired, because of the realistic costume of the participants as shown in this postcard. It is, of course, a clever reproduction put on in the Dunmow Pageant of 1912; the spectators in the background give the game away. It was the second section of a long day of pageantry; the 'Shakeshafts' have been closely questioned, but with the help of their counsel, acted by Lewis Coates and May Mills, they have won through, and the flitch is being borne aloft before them as their ultimate reward.

Jester & Hobby Horse with Morris Dancers. Dunmow Pageant.

76. The Pageant of 1912 seems a very good point at which to end this series of postcards, for here we see the good people of Dunmow in happy times celebrating and remembering the past glories of England in customary fun and games. The Great War was then only a small cloud on the politicians' horizon. Local identity, local crafts and self sufficiency were still strong in the Essex countryside. So there was no shortage of volunteers to make their own costumes and take humble parts in the grand design. Here, under the anxious eye of their schoolteacher, the girls all dressed in white, with kerchiefs at the ready, are about to lead off in a Morris dance. The jester in the foreground is riding the traditional hobby horse.